LEONARD BERN[STEIN]
ART SONGS AND ARIAS

29 SELECTIONS

Edited by Richard Walters
Editorial Consultants: Marie Carter, Garth Sunderland

ISBN-13: 978-1-4234-2753-7
ISBN-10: 1-4234-2753-X

LEONARD
BERNSTEIN
Music Publishing
Company LLC

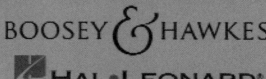

BOOSEY & HAWKES

HAL•LEONARD®

www.leonardbernstein.com
www.boosey.com
www.halleonard.com

TABLE OF CONTENTS

Songs

Arias

LEONARD BERNSTEIN
August 25, 1918 - October 14, 1990

Leonard Bernstein was born in Lawrence, Massachusetts. He took piano lessons as a boy and attended the Garrison and Boston Latin Schools. At Harvard University he studied with Walter Piston, Edward Burlingame-Hill, and A. Tillman Merritt, among others. Before graduating in 1939 he made an unofficial conducting debut with his own incidental music to *The Birds*, and directed and performed in Marc Blitzstein's *The Cradle Will Rock*. Subsequently, at the Curtis Institute of Music in Philadelphia, he studied piano with Isabella Vengerova, conducting with Fritz Reiner, and orchestration with Randall Thompson.

In 1940 he studied at the Boston Symphony Orchestra's newly created summer institute, Tanglewood, with the orchestra's conductor, Serge Koussevitzky. Bernstein later became Koussevitzky's conducting assistant.

Bernstein was appointed to his first permanent conducting post in 1943, as Assistant Conductor of the New York Philharmonic. On November 14, 1943, Bernstein substituted on a few hours notice for the ailing Bruno Walter at a Carnegie Hall concert, which was broadcast nationally on radio, receiving critical acclaim. Soon orchestras worldwide sought him out as a guest conductor.

In 1945 he was appointed Music Director of the New York City Symphony Orchestra, a post he held until 1947. After Serge Koussevitzky died in 1951, Bernstein headed the orchestral and conducting departments at Tanglewood, teaching there for many years. In 1951 he married the Chilean actress and pianist, Felicia Montealegre. He was also visiting music professor, and head of the Creative Arts Festivals at Brandeis University in the early 1950s.

Bernstein became Music Director of the New York Philharmonic in 1958. From then until 1969 he led more concerts with the orchestra than any previous conductor. He subsequently held the lifetime title of Laureate Conductor, making frequent guest appearances with the orchestra. Over half of Bernstein's more than 400 recordings were made with the New York Philharmonic.

Bernstein traveled the world as a conductor. Immediately after World War II, in 1946, he conducted in London and at the International Music Festival in Prague. In 1947 he conducted in Tel Aviv, beginning a relationship with Israel that lasted until his death. In 1953, Bernstein was the first American to conduct opera at the Teatro alla Scala in Milan in Cherubini's *Medea* with Maria Callas.

Bernstein was a leading advocate of American composers, particularly Aaron Copland. The two remained close friends for life. As a young pianist, Bernstein performed Copland's *Piano Variations* so often he considered the composition his trademark. Bernstein programmed and recorded nearly all of the Copland orchestral works — many of them twice. He devoted several televised *Young People's Concerts* to Copland, and gave the premiere of Copland's *Connotations*, commissioned for the opening of Philharmonic Hall (now Avery Fisher Hall) at Lincoln Center in 1962.

While Bernstein's conducting repertoire encompassed the standard literature, he may be best remembered for his performances and recordings of Haydn, Beethoven, Brahms, Schumann, Sibelius and Mahler. Particularly notable were his performances of the Mahler symphonies with the New York Philharmonic in the 1960s, sparking a renewed interest in the works of Mahler.

Inspired by his Jewish heritage, Bernstein completed his first large-scale work as a composer, Symphony No. 1: "Jeremiah." (1943). The piece was first performed with the Pittsburgh Symphony Orchestra in 1944, conducted by the composer, and received the New York Music Critics' Award. Koussevitzky premiered Bernstein's Symphony No. 2: "The Age of Anxiety" with the Boston Symphony Orchestra, with Bernstein as piano soloist. His Symphony No. 3: "Kaddish," composed in 1963, was premiered by the Israel Philharmonic Orchestra. "Kaddish" is dedicated "To the Beloved Memory of John F. Kennedy."

Other major compositions by Bernstein include *Prelude, Fugue and Riffs* for solo clarinet and jazz ensemble (1949); *Serenade* for violin, strings and percussion, (1954); *Symphonic Dances from West Side Story*, (1960); *Chichester Psalms* for chorus, boy soprano and orchestra (1965); *Mass: A Theater Piece for Singers, Players and Dancers*, commissioned for the opening of the John F. Kennedy Center for the Performing Arts in Washington, DC, and first produced there in 1971; *Songfest*, a song cycle for six singers and orchestra (1977); *Divertimento*, for orchestra (1980); *Halil*, for solo flute and small orchestra (1981); *Touches*, for solo piano (1981); *Missa Brevis* for singers and percussion (1988); *Thirteen Anniversaries* for solo piano (1988); *Concerto for Orchestra: Jubilee Games*, (1989); and *Arias and Barcarolles* for two singers and piano duet (1988).

Bernstein also wrote a one-act opera, *Trouble in Tahiti*, in 1952, and its sequel, the three-act opera, *A Quiet Place* in 1983. He collaborated with choreographer Jerome Robbins on three major ballets: *Fancy Free* (1944) and *Facsimile* (1946) for the American Ballet theater; and *Dybbuk* (1975) for the New York City Ballet. He composed the score for the award-winning movie *On the Waterfront* (1954) and incidental music for two Broadway plays: *Peter Pan* (1950) and *The Lark* (1955).

Bernstein contributed substantially to the Broadway musical stage. He collaborated with Betty Comden and Adolph Green on *On The Town* (1944) and *Wonderful Town* (1953). In collaboration with Richard Wilbur and Lillian Hellman and others he wrote *Candide* (1956). Other versions of *Candide* were written in association with Hugh Wheeler, Stephen Sondheim, et al. In 1957 he again collaborated with Jerome Robbins, Stephen Sondheim, and Arthur Laurents, on the landmark musical *West Side Story*, also made into the Academy Award-winning film. In 1976 Bernstein and Alan Jay Lerner wrote *1600 Pennsylvania Avenue*.

Festivals of Bernstein's music have been produced throughout the world. In 1978 the Israel Philharmonic sponsored a festival commemorating his years of dedication to Israel. The Israel Philharmonic also bestowed on him the lifetime title of Laureate Conductor in 1988. In 1986 the London Symphony Orchestra and the Barbican Centre produced a Bernstein Festival. The London Symphony Orchestra in 1987 named him Honorary President. In 1989 the city of Bonn presented a Beethoven/Bernstein Festival.

In 1985 the National Academy of Recording Arts and Sciences honored Mr. Bernstein with the Lifetime Achievement Grammy Award. He won eleven Emmy Awards in his career. His televised concert and lecture series started with the *Omnibus* program in 1954, followed by the extraordinary *Young People's Concerts with the New York Philharmonic* in 1958 that extended over fourteen seasons. Among his many appearances on the PBS series *Great Performances* was the eleven-part acclaimed "Bernstein's Beethoven." In 1989, Bernstein and others commemorated the 1939 invasion of Poland in a worldwide telecast from Warsaw.

Bernstein's writings were published in *The Joy of Music* (1959), *Leonard Bernstein's Young People's Concerts* (1961), *The Infinite Variety of Music* (1966), and *Findings* (1982). Each has been widely translated. He gave six lectures at Harvard University in 1972-1973 as the Charles Eliot Norton Professor of Poetry. These lectures were subsequently published and televised as *The Unanswered Question*.

Bernstein always rejoiced in opportunities to teach young musicians. His master classes at Tanglewood were famous. He was instrumental in founding the Los Angeles Philharmonic Institute in 1982. He helped create a world class training orchestra at the Schleswig Holstein Music Festival. He founded the Pacific Music Festival in Sapporo, Japan. Modeled after Tanglewood, this international festival was the first of its kind in Asia and continues to this day.

Bernstein received many honors. He was elected in 1981 to the American Academy of Arts and Letters, which gave him a Gold Medal. The National Fellowship Award in 1985 applauded his life-long support of humanitarian causes. He received the MacDowell Colony's Gold Medal; medals from the Beethoven Society and the Mahler Gesellschaft; the Handel Medallion, New York City's highest honor for the arts; a Tony award (1969) for Distinguished Achievement in the Theater; and dozens of honorary degrees and awards from colleges and universities. He was presented ceremonial keys to the cities of Oslo, Vienna, Bersheeva and the village of Bernstein, Austria, among others. National honors came from Italy, Israel, Mexico, Denmark, Germany (the Great Merit Cross), and France (Chevalier, Officer and Commandeur of the Legion d'Honneur). He received the Kennedy Center Honors in 1980.

World peace was a particular concern of Bernstein. Speaking at Johns Hopkins University in 1980 and the Cathedral of St. John the Divine in New York in 1983, he described his vision of global harmony. His "Journey for Peace" tour to Athens and Hiroshima with the European Community Orchestra in 1985, commemorated the 40th anniversary of the atom bomb. In December 1989 Bernstein conducted the historic "Berlin Celebration Concerts" on both sides of the Berlin Wall, as it was being dismantled. The concerts were unprecedented gestures of cooperation, the musicians representing the former East Germany, West Germany, and the four powers that had partitioned Berlin after World War II.

Bernstein supported Amnesty International from its inception. To benefit the effort in 1987, he established the Felicia Montealegre Fund in memory of his wife who died in 1978.

In 1990 Bernstein received the Praemium Imperiale, an international prize created in 1988 by the Japan Arts Association and awarded for lifetime achievement in the arts. Bernstein used the $100,000 prize to establish The Bernstein Education Through the Arts (BETA) Fund, Inc. before his death on October 14, 1990.

Bernstein was the father of three children — Jamie, Alexander, and Nina — and the grandfather of two: Francisca and Evan.

About the Selections

Songs

Afterthought

Composed 1945. Words by Leonard Bernstein. First known performance: October 24, 1948, Town Hall, New York, New York. Performers: Nell Tangeman, soprano; Robert Cornman, piano. Dedication: "In memory of HJR." "Afterthought" was as a study for the ballet *Facsimile*, a commission from Ballet Theatre, choreographed by Jerome Robbins; Bernstein conducted the ballet premiere on October 24, 1946 at the Broadway Theatre, New York, New York. "Afterthought" was also orchestrated in 1945 as part of the compositional study for the ballet; performance materials are available on rental from Boosey & Hawkes.

from *Arias and Barcarolles*
Little Smary
Greeting

Composed 1988. *Arias and Barcarolles* is a cycle of songs for mezzo-soprano, baritone and piano/four hands, with words by Leonard Bernstein for all but two songs, including "Little Smary" by Jennie Bernstein, the composer's mother. The original version, for four singers (soprano, mezzo-soprano, two baritones), was premiered on May 9, 1988, Equitable Center Auditorium, New York, New York. Performers: Louise Edeiken, soprano, Joyce Castle, mezzo-soprano, John Brandstetter, baritone, Mordechai Kaston, baritone, Leonard Bernstein and Michael Tilson Thomas, piano. The first performance of the revised version for two singers was on April 28, 1989, Museum of Art, Tel Aviv, Israel. Performers: Amalia Ishak, soprano, Raphael Frieder, baritone, Irit Rub-Levy and Ariel Cohen, piano. First American performance of the revised version: September 7, 1989, Merkin Concert Hall, New York, New York. Performers: Judy Kaye, soprano, William Sharp, baritone, Michael Barrett and Steven Blier, piano.

Orchestrated in 1988, with the assistance of Bright Sheng, for strings and percussion. First performance of the orchestrated version: September 22, 1989, Tilles Center, Long Island University, New York. Performers: Susan Graham, mezzo-soprano, Kurt Ollmann, baritone, New York Chamber Symphony, Gerard Schwartz, conductor. A second orchestrated version for full orchestra, orchestrations by Bruce Coughlin, was premiered on September 26, 1993, Barbican Centre, London, England. Performers: Frederica von Stade, mezzo-soprano, Thomas Hampson, baritone, London Symphony Orchestra, Michael Tilson Thomas, conductor. Score and parts for both orchestrated versions are available on rental from Boosey & Hawkes. Vocal score, published by Boosey & Hawkes, available for sale.

from Jack Gottlieb's "Prefatory Note" in the vocal score:

> *Arias and Barcarolles* is a both a memory piece and a rumination on the nature of love…The main title and the dedications are based on the composer-conductor's personal experiences; but the life cycle events recalled are universal, though not necessarily sung in chronological order: birth ("Greeting"), infancy ("Little Smary"), the mystery of creativity in conflict with mundane affairs ("Love Duet"), inconclusive liaisons ("The Love of My Life"), wedding ("Oif Mayn Khas'neh"), married life ("Mr. and Mrs. Webb Say Goodnight"), and death ("Nachspiel").

> On April 5, 1960, Maestro Bernstein appeared as pianist-conductor with members of the New York Philharmonic in a concert of the Mozart *Piano Concerto in G Major, K. 453,* and Gershwin's *Rhapsody in Blue* at the White House. Afterwards, President Eisenhower said to Mr. Bernstein: "I liked that last piece you played. It's got a theme. I like music with a theme, not all them [sic] arias and barcarolles." This artless phrasing imbedded itself in the composer's memory to be recalled twenty-eight years later, in 1988.

> The terms "arias" and "barcarolles" are, of course, most often associated with high-brow European opera. Therefore, Eisenhower's ingenuous commentary was a low-brow American suspicion of European musical traditions. *Arias and Barcarolles*, nevertheless, wryly and resolutely makes use of the European art-song tradition…

> "Little Smary" by Jennie Bernstein is a recollection of a story often told to the composer by his mother when he was a child…When the Bernstein's son, Alexander Serge, was born in 1955, the proud father wrote "Greeting" (revised in 1988) as a kind of thanksgiving prayer.

La Bonne Cuisine
Four Recipes
> **Plum Pudding**
> **Queues de Bœuf (Ox-Tails)**
> **Tavouk Gueunksis**
> **Civet à Toute Vitesse (Rabbit at Top Speed)**

Composed 1947. Words are recipes from *La Bonne Cuisine Française* by Emile Dutoit (in French), English versions by Leonard Bernstein. First performance: October 10, 1948, Town Hall, New York, New York. Performers: Marion Bell, soprano, Edwin MacArthur, piano.

Dedication: "To Jennie Tourel," born Belarus, 1900, died New York, 1973, a mezzo-soprano closely associated with Bernstein and his music. Tourel's opera career was primarily in Italian coloratura roles. She was the first performer of Baba the Turk in *The Rake's Progress*.

from notes by Jack Gottlieb in the Bernstein *Song Album* (Boosey & Hawkes):

> Émile Dumont's *La Bonne Cuisine Française (Tout ce qui a Rapport a la Table, Manuel-Guide pour la Ville et la Campagne)* "Fine French Cooking (Everything That Has to Do with the Table, Manual Guide for City and Country)," was first published in 1899. "Plum Pudding," adapted by the composer from a larger recipe, appears under "Mets Anglais" (English Dishes). "Queues de Bœuf" (Ox-Tails) is taken whole. "Tavouk Gueunksis," a Turkish delight, is also complete, and comes from the section "Patisserie et Confiserie Turques" (Turkish Pastries and Sweets). Two ingredients of the original recipe are missing from the musical setting of "Civet à Toute Vitesse" (Rabbit at Top Speed): *muscade* (nutmeg) and *un verre d'eau-de-vie* (a glass of brandy).

> *Literal Translations by Ron Mendelssohn:*

> Plum Pudding

> 250 grams of Malaga grapes, 250 grams of Corinth grapes; (Corinth grapes); 250 grams of beef kidney fat, and 125 grams of bread crumbs; (of bread crumbs!). 60 grams of powdered or brown sugar; a glass of milk; a half glass of rum or brandy; 3 eggs; a lemon! powdered nutmeg, ginger, cinnamon, mixed (all together about half a teaspoon); half a teaspoon of finely ground salt.

> Queues de Bœuf (Ox-Tails)

> Ox-tails is not a dish to be scorned. First of all, with enough ox-tails you can make a tolerable stew. The tails that were used to make the stew can be eaten, breaded, and broiled, and served with hot or tomato sauce. Ox-tails is not a dish to be scorned.

> Tavouk Gueunksis

> Tavouk Gueunksis, breast of hen; put a hen to boil, and take the white meat and chop it into shreds. Mix it with a broth, like the one for Mahallebi. Tavouk Gueunksis, breast of hen.

> Civet à Toute Vitesse (Rabbit at Top Speed)

> Should you be in a hurry, here's a method for preparing rabbit stew that I recommend! Cut up the rabbit (hare) as for an ordinary stew: put it in a pot with its blood and liver mashed. A half pound of breast of pork, chopped; twenty or so small onions (a dash of salt and pepper); a liter and a half of red wine. Bring this quickly to boil. After about fifteen minutes, when the sauce is reduced to half of what it was, apply a fire, to set the stew aflame. When the fire goes out, add to the sauce half a pound of butter, worked with flour... and serve.

I Hate Music!

A Cycle of Five Kid Songs

    I. My Name Is Barbara
    II. Jupiter Has Seven Moons
    III. I Hate Music!
    IV. A Big Indian and a Little Indian
    V. I'm a Person Too

Composed fall of 1942 into 1943. Words by Leonard Bernstein. First performance: August 24, 1943, Public Library, Lennox, Massachusetts. Performers: Jennie Tourel, mezzo-soprano, Leonard Bernstein, piano. Dedicated to Edys Merrill, artist, friend and flatmate of Bernstein in the 1940s, because, apparently, she used to emphatically exclaim the title phrase as Bernstein made much noise coaching singers and playing the piano.

Humphrey Burton, in his book *Leonard Bernstein*, stated that the composer confessed to to his friend Aaron Copland that *I Hate Music!* was "a little on the Copland side." Copland wrote back, "I want to hear about your writing a song that has no Copland, no Hindemith, no Strav., no Bloch, no Milhaud and no Bartók in it. Then I'll talk to you." The most unusual recording of this music is by Barbra Streisand, who sang "My Name Is Barbara" and "I Hate Music!"

My Twelve-Tone Melody

Words by Leonard Bernstein. Composed shortly before the first performance on May 11, 1988, Carnegie Hall, New York, New York, a concert celebrating the 100th birthday of Irving Berlin. The end of the song quotes Berlin's 1925 hit "Always." Unpublished prior to this collection.

Piccola Serenata

Composed August 25, 1979 (Bernstein's birthday) to honor conductor Karl Boehm's 85th birthday. Words by Leonard Bernstein (nonsense syllables). First performance: August 27, 1979, Salzburg, Austria. Performers: Christa Ludwig, mezzo-soprano, James Levine, piano.

Silhouette (Galilee)

Composed 1951. Words by Leonard Bernstein, incorporating a Lebanese folksong. First performance: February 13, 1955, National Gallery of Art, Washington, DC. Performers: Katherine Hanse, mezzo-soprano, Evelyn Swarthout, piano. Later orchestrated by Sid Ramin. Full score and parts are available on rental from Boosey & Hawkes.

from *Songfest*

    A Julia de Burgos
    Music I Heard With You
    Zizi's Lament

Composed September 1976 into 1977. A cycle of American poems for six singers (soprano, mezzo-soprano, alto, tenor, baritone, bass) and orchestra. Dedication: "For My Mother" (Jennie Resnick Bernstein, 1898-1992). First performance of four songs in the set, including the three in this collection: November 24, 1976, Avery Fisher Hall, New York, New York. Performers: Victoria Canale, soprano, Elaine Bonazzi, mezzo-soprano, Florence Quivar, mezzo-soprano, John Reardon, baritone, the New York Philharmonic, Leonard Bernstein, conductor. First performance of the complete work: October 11, 1977, the Kennedy Center, Washington, DC. Performers: Clamma Dale, soprano, Rosalind Elias, mezzo-soprano, Nancy Williams, mezzo-soprano, Neil Rosenshein, tenor, John Reardon, baritone, Donald Gramm, bass-baritone, the National Symphony Orchestra, Leonard Bernstein, conductor. This cast was recorded by Deutsche Grammophon. Vocal score, published by Boosey & Hawkes, for sale. Full score and parts in original and reduced orchestration available on rental from Boosey & Hawkes.

"A Julia de Burgos," words by the Puerto Rican poet Julia de Burgos (1917-1953). "Music I Heard With You," poem by Conrad Aiken (1889-1973). "Zizi's Lament," poem by Gregory Corso (b. 1930), one of the Beat writers of the 1950s.

A Julia de Burgos

Bernstein set only the first half of the poem.
translation by Jamie Bernstein

To Julia de Burgos

Ya las gentes murmuran que yo soy tu enemiga
porque dicen que en verso doy al mundo tu yo.

The talk's around that I wish you ill
because, they say, through verse I give the world your I.

Mienten, Julia de Burgos. Mienten, Julia de Burgos.
La que se alza en mis versos no es tu voz: es mi voz;
porque tú eres ropaje y la escencia soy yo;
y el más profundo abismo se tiende entre las dos.

They lie, Julia de Burgos. They lie, Julia de Burgos.
What rises from my lines is not your voice: it's my voice.
For you are but drapery; the essence is I,
and between those two the deepest chasm lies.

Tú eres fría muñeca de mentira social,
y yo, viril destello de la humana verdad.

You are the frosty doll of social deceit,
and I, a virile flash of human truth.

Tú, miel de cortesanas hipocresías; yo no;
que todos mis poemas desnudo el corazón.

You are the syrup of genteel hypocrisy; not me.
In every poem I strip my heart bare.

Tú eres como tu mundo, egoísta; yo no;
que en todo me lo juego a ser lo que soy yo.

You are selfish, like your universe; not me.
I gamble it all to be exactly as I am.

Tú eres sólo la grave señora señorona; yo no,
yo soy la vida, la fuerza, la mujer.

You are that oh so lofty lady of consequence; not me.
I am the life, the power, the woman.

Tú eres de tu marido, de tu amo; yo no;
yo de nadie, o de todos, porque a todos,
a todos en mi limpio sentir y en mi pensar me doy.

You are the property of your spouse, your boss; not me.
I'm no one's, or everyone's, for to every single one
through my cleansed senses, through my thoughts I offer myself.

Tú te rizas el pelo y te pintas; yo no;
a mí me riza el viento, a mí me pinta el sol.

You curl your hair and paint your face; not me.
I get the wind to curl me, the sun to paint me.

Tú eres dama casera, resignada, sumisa,
atada a los prejuicios de los hombres; yo no;
que yo soy Rocinante corriendo desbocado
olfateando horizontes de justicia de Dios.

Housebound lady, you are resigned, compliant,
bound to the bigotries of men; not me.
For I am runaway Rosinante, unbridled,
sniffing out horizons of the justice of God.

Courtesy of Consuelo Burgos Garcia on behalf of the Estate of Julia de Burgos.
English translation © 1977 by Jamie Bernstein.

Songfest was originally commissioned for the bicentennial by the Philadelphia Orchestra, but Bernstein delayed work at the time, instead turning his attention to *1600 Pennsylvania Avenue*. The selection of texts, deliberately representing diverse poetic voices, stress diversity in American culture, as do the mix of musical styles in the piece.

Two Love Songs
Extinguish my eyes
When my soul touches yours

Composed 1949. Poems by Rainer Maria Rilke (1875-1926). English translations by Jessie Lemont. "Extinguish my eyes" first performed March 13, 1949, Town Hall, New York, New York. Performers (?): Jennie Tourel, mezzo-soprano, Leonard Bernstein, piano. "When my soul touches yours" first performed March 13, 1963, Philharmonic Hall, New York, New York. Performers: Jennie Tourel, mezzo-soprano, Alan Rogers, piano. Orchestrated by Sid Ramin; score and parts available on rental from Boosey & Hawkes.

Arias

from *Candide*
Glitter and Be Gay

Composed 1956. Comic operetta in two acts. Original version withdrawn by the composer (not available for performance). Book by Lillian Hellman (after Voltaire), lyrics by Richard Wilbur, John LaTouche, Dorothy Parker, Lillian Hellman, Leonard Bernstein. First performance: October 29, 1956, Colonial Theater, Boston, Massachusetts; directed by Tyrone Guthrie; Samuel Krachmalnick, conductor. Orchestration by Leonard Bernstein and Hershy Kay. Broadway opening: December 1, 1956, Martin Beck Theater, New York, New York. Principal cast: Robert Rounseville (Candide), Barbara Cook (Cunegonde), Max Adrian (Dr. Pangloss/Martin), Irra Petina (Old Lady), William Olvis (Governor), Louis Edmunds (Maximilian).

"Chelsea Version" 1973. Comic operetta in one act. Book: Hugh Wheeler (after Voltaire), lyrics: Richard Wilbur, John LaTouche, Stephen Sondheim, Leonard Bernstein. Orchestration for 13 players: Hershy Kay First performance: December 20, 1973, Chelsea Theater, Brooklyn, New York; directed by Harold Prince; John Mauceri, conductor. Broadway opening: March 5, 1974, Broadway Theater, New York, New York.

"New York City Opera Version" 1982. Comic Operetta in two acts. Book: Hugh Wheeler (after Voltaire). Lyrics: Richard Wilbur, John LaTouche, Stephen Sondheim, Leonard Bernstein. Orchestrations: Leonard Bernstein, Hershy Kay and John Mauceri. First performance: October 13, 1982, New York City Opera.

"Scottish Opera Version" (revised Opera House version) 1988. Comic operetta in two acts. Book: Hugh Wheeler (after Voltaire), lyrics: Richard Wilbur, Stephen Sondheim, John LaTouche, Lillian Hellman, Dorothy Parker, Leonard Bernstein. First performance: May 17, 1988, Theatre Royal, Glasgow, Scotland. Edition by John Wells and John Mauceri (also conductor). Orchestration: same as in New York City Opera House Version. Study score, vocal score, vocal selections, published by Boosey & Hawkes, for sale.

From the vocal score of *Candide* (Scottish Opera Version), edited by Charles Harmon:

> The engraving of this score is based on Leonard Bernstein's conducting score for his 1989 Deutsche Grammophon recording of *Candide*, as well as the orchestra material used in that recording, and the manuscripts of Leonard Bernstein at the Library of Congress.

The selection from *Candide* in this collection uses the published vocal score (Scottish Opera Version) as a source.

Glitter and Be Gay
from Act I, scene 7
character: Cunegonde Thunder-ten-Tronck
setting: Cunegonde's room, Paris, 18th century

Cunegonde was once an innocent German girl of Westphalia in love with Candide. War and bad fortune dealt hardship to her and her family, but she has survived in Paris as the well-kept mistress of, simultaneously, the Archbishop, and the wealthy Jew, Don Issachar. Cunegonde has developed a strong taste for the luxury given to her by her benefactors, apparent in this witty spin on the operatic tradition of a "jewel song." She undresses for the evening as she sings, commenting on her "fallen state" while removing her finery and jewelry with the help of her maid servant, known simply as the Old Lady.

from *Mass*
> **A Simple Song**
> **Thank You**
> **The Word of the Lord**
> **Hurry**
> **World Without End**
> **Our Father… I Go On**

"A Theatre Piece for Singers, Players and Dancers." Words are from the liturgy of the Roman Mass, with additional texts by Stephen Schwartz and Leonard Bernstein. Orchestration by Jonathan Tunick, Hershy Kay and Leonard Bernstein. Composed for opening of the John F. Kennedy Center for the Performing Arts, Washington, D.C. Dedication: "For Roger L. Stevens," theatrical producer, longtime Bernstein supporter, and chairman and artistic director of the Kennedy Center. First performance: September 8, 1971, Kennedy Center, Washington, DC. Directed by Gordon Davidson, choreographed by Alvin Ailey. Principal performers of the selections in this collection: Alan Titus, Lee Hooper, Gina Penn, Mary Bracken Phillips, Maurice Peress, conductor. The composer conducted the recording released in 1971. The vocal score, published by Boosey & Hawkes, is available for sale. Chamber version, orchestrated by Sid Ramin, first performed December 26, 1972, Mark Taper Forum, Los Angeles, California. Performance materials for both the original and chamber versions are available on rental from Boosey & Hawkes.

Editor's note: Some of the solo singing roles in *Mass* are for rock/theatre voices; others are for classical voices. *Art Songs and Arias* includes the classical selections only, and transposed as appropriate for either High Voice or Medium/Low Voice. Other selections from *Mass*, in a rock/theatre style, are published in *Bernstein Theatre Songs*.

Mass is an abstract, contemporary spiritual journey of doubts and affirmations in the context of the ritual of the traditional liturgy. It was composed for singers in various musical styles: chorus, a traditional boys choir, a stage orchestra, a pit orchestra, a rock band, and pre-recorded sound. "A Simple Song" (a Hymn and Psalm) is sung by the Mass celebrant (a high lyric baritone) at the beginning of the show in the Devotions Before Mass section. "Thank You," sung by a soprano soloist, is a trope in the Gloria section (IV). "The Word of the Lord" is an Epistle (section VIII), sung by the Celebrant with chorus. "Hurry" and "World Without End" are tropes from the Credo section (X), both sung by a mezzo-soprano soloist. "World Without End" is sung by a theatre soprano on the recording conducted by Bernstein. She belts sections of the song; a classical singer could sing it with a different approach. After "Hurry" there is a brief recorded chorus (Sedet ad dexteram Patris. Et iterum venturus est cum Gloria judicare vivos et mortuos: Cujus regni non erit finis), then the mezzo-soprano continues with "World Without End." After a disruption in the service, in The Lord's Prayer section (XIII) the Celebrant is left alone before preparing for communion and sings "Our Father" and "I Go On."

from *A Quiet Place*
   I've been afraid
   Mommy, are you here (Dede's Aria)

Opera in three acts. Libretto by Stephen Wadsworth and Leonard Bernstein. Orchestrations by Irwin Kostal, Sid Ramin and Leonard Bernstein. Commissioned by Houston Grand Opera, Kennedy Center and Teatro Alla Scala. Dedication: "To the Memory of F.M.B. and N.S.Z." First version (withdrawn, sequel to *Trouble in Tahiti*) first performed June 17, 1983 at Houston Grand Opera. Principal performers: Theodor Uppman (Bill), Dana Krueger (Susie), Douglas Perry (Analyst), Peter Harrower (Doc), Carolyne James (Mrs. Doc), Sheri Greenawald (Dede), Peter Kazaras (François), Timothy Nolen (Junior), Chester Ludgin (Sam), John DeMain, conductor. Revised version (incorporates *Trouble in Tahiti*) first performed June 19, 1984 at La Scala, Milan. Vocal score, published by Boosey & Hawkes, is available for sale. Full score and parts are available on rental from Boosey & Hawkes.

Bernstein's one-act opera *Trouble in Tahiti* (1951) was the starting point for the characters in *A Quiet Place*, which takes place three decades later. In the revised version of the opera *Trouble in Tahiti* is incorporated as flashbacks.

Family and friends have gathered for the funeral of Dinah, mother to Dede and Junior, somewhere in "Suburban America." François (tenor) is married to Dede. In Act II, scene 3 François, Junior's former lover, has just come from a harrowing scene with him. François finds Dede in the hallway and declares his love for her. François is French-Canadian and sings in a mixture of English and French. As Act III begins Dede is in her mother's once beautiful but now neglected garden. She feels her dead mother's presence and sings to her.

SONGS

In Memoriam: H.J.R.

Afterthought

Study for the ballet "Facsimile"

original key

Words and Music by
LEONARD BERNSTEIN

heart's child: the wide-eyed heart's child nev - er will cry: The

love un - spo - ken can - not be a lie!

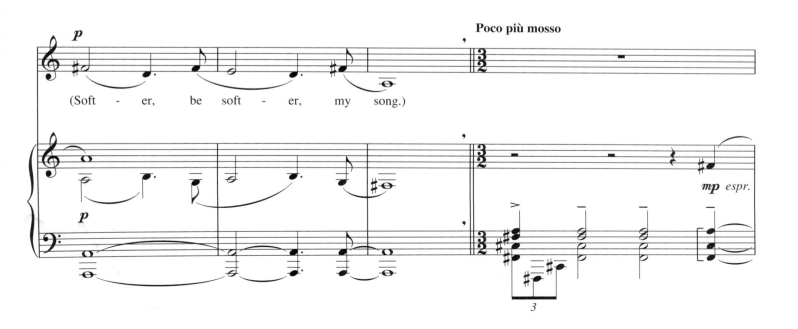

(Soft - er, be soft - er, my song.)

Poco più mosso

And though we may send up a tim - id leaf, a ten - der bough,

We rise too late to greet our un - known

loves.

May 1, 1945

For S.A.B.

Little Smary
from ARIAS AND BARCAROLLES
original key

Words by
JENNIE BERNSTEIN

Music by
LEONARD BERNSTEIN

N.B. The song is to be performed very seriously throughout, not "cute." - L.B.

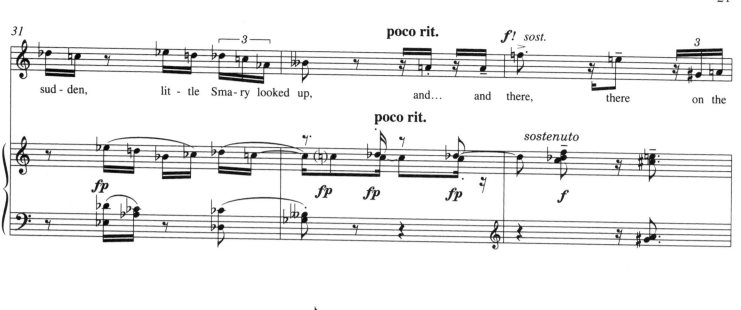

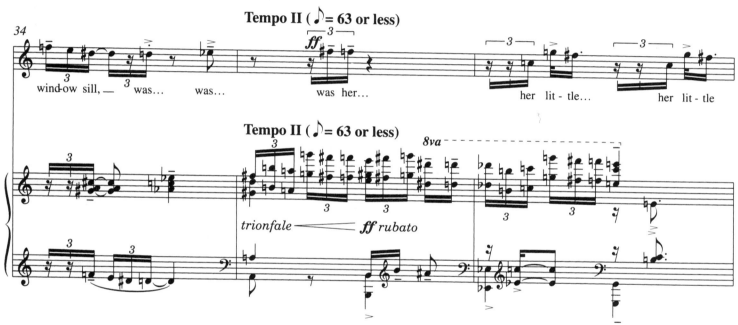

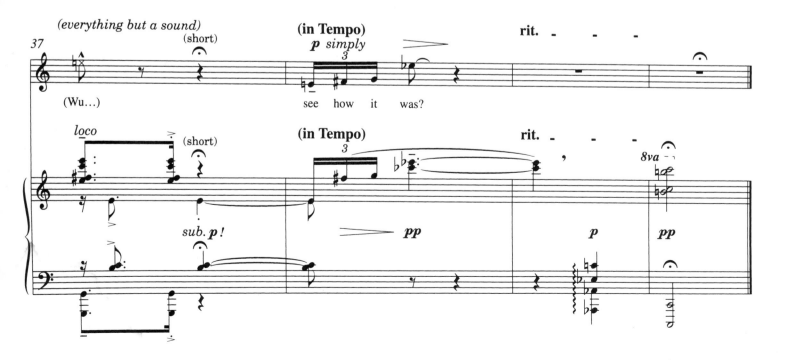

For J.G.

Greeting
from ARIAS AND BARCAROLLES
original key: a minor third lower

Words and Music by
LEONARD BERNSTEIN

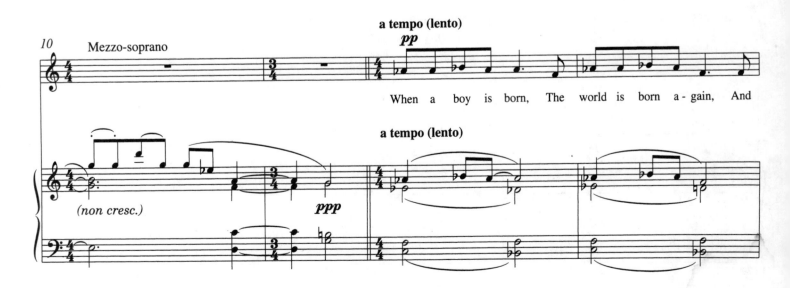

When a boy is born, The world is born a-gain, And

For Edys

I Hate Music!
A Cycle of Five Kid Songs

(In the performance of these songs, coyness is to be assiduously avoided. The natural, unforced sweetness of child expressions can never be successfully gilded; rather will it come through the music in proportion to the dignity and sophisticated understanding of the singer.)

original key

Words and Music by
LEONARD BERNSTEIN

I. My Name is Barbara

II. Jupiter Has Seven Moons

III. I Hate Music!

IV. A Big Indian and a Little Indian

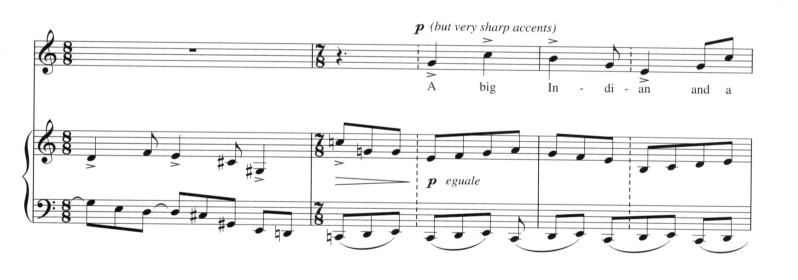

V. I'm a Person Too

But ev-'ry-one says, "Is-n't she cute? She likes bal-loons!"

Tempo I *(recovering assertiveness)*

I'm a per - son too, like you!

Tempo II *(simply, by way of explanation)*

I like things that ev-'ry-one likes: I like soft things and mov-ies and hors-es and

warm things and red things: don't you?

Tempo I

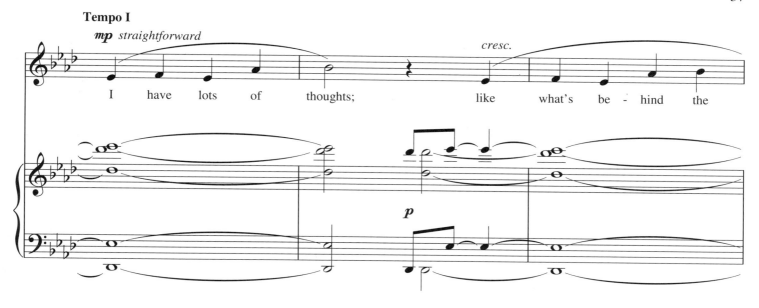

I have lots of thoughts; like what's be - hind the

sky; and what's be - hind what's be - hind the sky: But

Tempo II

ev -'ry-one says, "Is - n't she sweet? She wants to know ev -'ry-thing!" Don't you? Of

Tempo I

suddenly a little bit unsure   *cresc.*

course I'm ver - y young to be say - ing all these

gradually recovering assertiveness

things in front of so man - y peo - ple like you; but

Meno mosso

with dignity

I'm a per - son too! Though I'm on - ly

ten years old; I'm a per - son too, like you!

New York City
March, 1943

For Jennie Tourel
The only begetter of these songs

La Bonne Cuisine
Four Recipes
original key

Texts from
"La Bonne Cuisine Francaise"
by Émile Dumont
English version by L.B.

Music by
LEONARD BERNSTEIN

I. Plum Pudding

verr' de lait; un de-mi verr' de rhum ou d'eau-de-vi - e; trois oeufs; un cit-
glass of milk, and half a glass of Ba-car-di or brand-y; three eggs, and a

ron! _____
lem - on.

Mus - ca - de, gin-gem-bre, can-nell' en
Now mustard, powdered cin-na-mon, and

poud-re, mé-lan-gés (en tout la moi-tié d'un-e cuil-lè-re à
gin-ger, all to-geth-er mak-ing half a tea-spoon-ful of con-di-

ca-fé;) sel fin la moi-tié d'un-e cuil-lè-re à ca-fé.
ment which you com-bine with half a tea-spoon-ful of ta-ble salt.

II. Queues de Bœuf
(Ox-Tails)

boeuf _____ n'est pas un mets à dé - dai - gner. _____
proud _____ to serve your friends an ox - tail stew? _____

D'a - bord _____ a - vec as - sez de
You're wrong! _____ For if you have e-

III. Tavouk Gueunksis

IV. Civet à Toute Vitesse
(Rabbit at Top Speed)

Dé - pe - cez le lièv - re com - me pour le ci - vet or - di - naire:
Take a - part the rab - bit in the or - di - na - ry way you do.

p, come sopra

Met - tez - le dans u - ne cas - se - ro - le ou un chaud - ron a -
Put it in a pot or in a cas - se - role, or a bowl with

vec son sang et son foie é - cra - sé!
all its blood and with its liv - er mashed.

f, sim.

r. h.

mp, legato

Un' de - mi - liv - re de poi - tri - ne de porc (cou-pée en mor-ceaux);
Take half a pound of breast of pork, fine - ly cut (as fine as pos-si - ble);

p

My Twelve-Tone Melody

Music and Lyrics by
LEONARD BERNSTEIN

55

*In his manuscript Bernstein indicated "ad lib. 12-tone" to the end in the piano part. This version is just an editorial suggestion.

"Always"
Words and Music by Irving Berlin
© Copyright 1925 by Irving Berlin
Used by Permission.

For Karl Boehm
Piccola Serenata
original key: a whole step lower

Music and Lyrics by
LEONARD BERNSTEIN

For Jennie Tourel, on her birthday in Israel

Silhouette

(Galilee)

original key

Words and Music by
LEONARD BERNSTEIN

Allegretto, molto ritmico ♩ = 108

A last lit-tle bird on a palm feath-er rid - ing,

Black and clean in the af - ter - glow. _____ A

lone lit-tle girl in the ol-ive grove hid - ing, Croon-ing soft as the

sun sinks low: oo, oo,

oo, oo. Hu! hu! *'rr - fáh!

**oo,

oo! An old lit - tle jeep through the

*The "rr" should be rolled with the tongue.
**If "oo" is too difficult in this register, "ah" may be sung instead.

moun - tains _ crawl - ing, Tough and ti - ny a - gainst _ the _ sun, _____

_____ A young Ar - ab shep - herd up - on his knees _ fall - ing,

Al - lah, Al - lah, the day _____ is _____ done, _____ ee, _____

ee, _____ ee, _____ ee: _____

sub. ff

lips — a - trem - ble, Drunk with love and the chant they — sing: Wa -

molto f

lad el - a *'U - na, wa - lad —— el - a 'U — na,

Nor - kod **taht el ze - tu —— na! Wa -

lad el - a 'U - na, wa - lad —— el - a 'U — na,

*The "U" is to be pronounced gutturally, deep in the throat.
**The "h" in "taht" is highly aspirated.

A Julia de Burgos
from SONGFEST
original key

Poem by
JULIA DE BURGOS

Music by
LEONARD BERNSTEIN

Ya las gen-tes mur -

mur-an que yo soy tu e-ne-mi-ga_____

voz: es mi voz; es mi voz; es mi voz;

por-que tú e-res ro-pa-je y la-e-scen-cia soy yo;

y el más pro-fun-do a-

bis - mo se tien - de en-tre las dos.

Tú e-res frí-a mu - ñe-ca de men - ti - ra so - cial,

— y yo, vi - ril de-ste - llo de la hu - ma - na ver -

dad. _____ Tú,

miel de cor - te - sa - nas hi - po - cre - sí - as; yo no; _____

que en to - dos mis po - e - mas des - nu - do el co - ra -

Duration: 3'27"

Zizi's Lament
from SONGFEST
original key

Poem by
GREGORY CORSO

Music by
LEONARD BERNSTEIN

never had the laugh - (ha ha ha ha) ing sick - ness,

so what good am I?

The fat mer-chant

Duration: 2'27"

Music I Heard With You
from SONGFEST
original key

Poem by
CONRAD AIKEN

Music by
LEONARD BERNSTEIN

Mu-sic I heard with you was more than mu-sic, And

bread I broke with you was more than bread;____ Now that I am with-

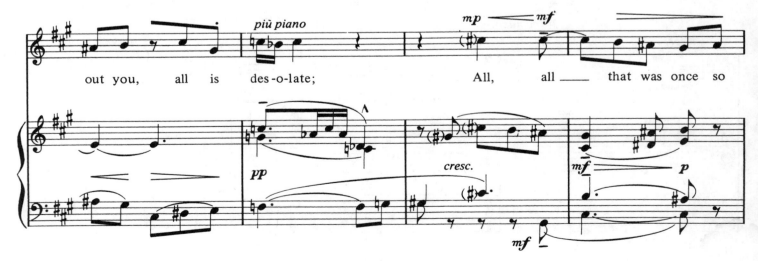

out you, all is des-o-late; All, all ____ that was once so

Duration: 3′24″

Two Love Songs
I. Extinguish my eyes...
original key

Poems by
RAINER MARIA RILKE
English translations by
Jessie Lemont

Music by
LEONARD BERNSTEIN

Poems used by permission of Columbia University Press.

cur - rents of my blood:

mf warm

Mm (humming)

pp possibile

(long as possible)

(repeat until voice is out)

Feb. 2, 1949

II. When my soul touches yours

original key

When my soul touch- es yours a great chord sings:

How can I tune it then to oth- er things? Oh, _____

_____ if some spot in dark- ness could be found That does not vi- brate when your

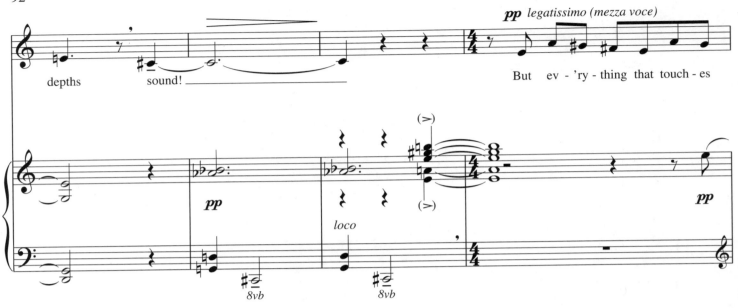

depths sound! But ev - 'ry - thing that touch - es

you and me welds us as played strings sound one mel-o - dy.

Where, where is the in - stru - ment whence the sounds

Feb. 4, 1949

ARIAS

Glitter and Be Gay
from CANDIDE
original key

Lyrics by
RICHARD WILBUR

Music by
LEONARD BERNSTEIN

Tempo di Valse Lente

Forced to bend my soul To a sor-did role,

Vic-tim-ized by bit-ter, _____ bit-ter cir-cum-stance. A-

Un poco animato *rall.*

las for me! ___ Had I re-mained Be-side my la-dy mo-ther, My

a tempo *cresc.* *rall.*

vir - tue had ___ re-mained un-stained Un-til my maid-en hand was

gained By some Grand Duke or oth-er.

Ah, 'twas not to be; Harsh ne-ces-si-ty

Brought me to this gild-ed cage.

Born to high-er things, Here I droop my wings, Ah!

Sing-ing of a sor-row no-thing can as-suage.

And yet, of course, I rath-er like to rev-el, ha ha! I have no strong ob-jec-tion to cham-pagne, ha ha! My ward-robe is ex-pen-sive as the

Take the place of Honor lost?   Can they compensate For my fallen state,   Purchased as they were

at such an awful cost?   Bracelets...lavallieres...   Can they dry   Can they blind
my tears?

my eyes to shame? Can the brightest brooch Shield me from reproach? Can the purest diamond purify my

Allegro molto, come prima

name?   And   yet,   of course, these trin‑kets are en‑dear‑ing,   ha ha!   I'm

Allegro molto, come prima

* Downbeat may be omitted in soprano.

A Simple Song
from MASS
original key

Lyrics by
STEPHEN SCHWARTZ and
LEONARD BERNSTEIN

Music by
LEONARD BERNSTEIN

Poco meno mosso (♩ = 88)

Cadenza (freely)

Lau - da, Lau - da, Lau - dē,   Lau - da,   Lau - da di da di   day...

A tempo (più lento)

All of my days.

Flute
A Simple Song
from MASS
original key

Lyrics by
**STEPHEN SCHWARTZ and
LEONARD BERNSTEIN**

Music by
LEONARD BERNSTEIN

This part may be carefully cut from the book.

The Word of the Lord
from MASS
original key

Lyrics by
STEPHEN SCHWARTZ and
LEONARD BERNSTEIN

Music by
LEONARD BERNSTEIN

loud, _____ Oh they bel-low and they blus-ter 'til they mus-ter up a crowd. _____

They can fash-ion a re-but-tal that's as sub-tle as a

sword, _____ But they're nev-er gon-na scut-tle the Word of the

Lord. _____

No, they're nev-er gon-na scut-tle ____ the Word of the

Lord! _____

All you

big men of mer-it, _____ (t)

all _____ you big men of mer-it who fer-ret out

grow - ing! _____ O you peo-ple of pow-er, _____ O _____ you

peo-ple of pow-er, your hour _ is now. _ You may plan to rule for-ev-er, but you nev-er do some-

how! _____ So we

* *Tremolo always at the same speed, regardless of rit. or* ⌢

Thank You
from MASS
original key

Lyrics by
STEPHEN SCHWARTZ and
LEONARD BERNSTEIN

Music by
LEONARD BERNSTEIN

Meno mosso (Moderato) ♩ = 72

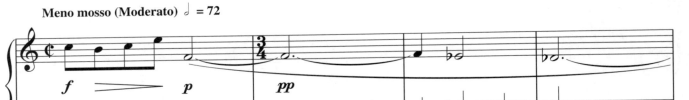

friend and a pil - low, A lov - er whose eyes Could

mir - ror my cries of Glo - ri - a...

And now, it's strange

Hurry
from MASS
original key

Lyrics by
STEPHEN SCHWARTZ and
LEONARD BERNSTEIN

Music by
LEONARD BERNSTEIN

While they got ___ a bit rough - er, Tough - er ___ and tough - er.

Well, things ___ are tough ___ e - nough. _____ So

♪ = ♪ (but a bit more urgent, moving forward)

(almost whispered)

when's your next ap - pear - ance on the scene? I'm read - y.

Hur - ry. Went to church for clear-ance and I'm clean And

stead - y. Hur - ry. While I'm wait-ing I can get my

bags packed, Flags flown, Shoes blacked,

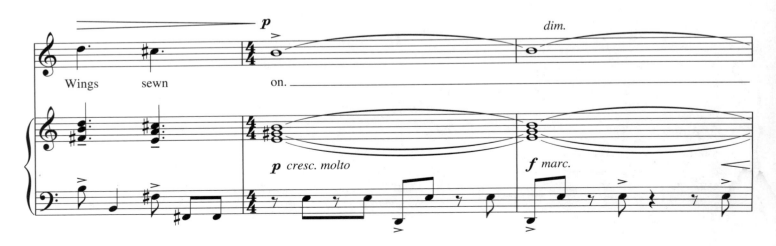

Wings sewn on.

World Without End
from MASS
original key

Lyrics by
STEPHEN SCHWARTZ and
LEONARD BERNSTEIN

Music by
LEONARD BERNSTEIN

136

Lord, don't you know it's the end of the world? Lord, don't you care if it

all ends to-day? Some-times I'd swear that you planned it this way...

Dark are the cit-ies, dead is the o-cean, Si - lent and sick-ly are the

rem - nants of mo - tion. World with - out end turns mind - less - ly round,

non cresc.

Nev - er a sen - try, nev - er a sound. No one to proph - e - sy dis -

cresc. un poco

as - ter, No one to help it hap - pen fast - er.

cresc. un poco

No one to ex-pe-dite the fall, _____ No one to soil the breeze,

No one to oil the seas, No one to an-y-thing,

No one to an-y-thing, No one to an-y-thing at all.

Our Father...I Go On
from MASS
original key

Lyrics by
STEPHEN SCHWARTZ and
LEONARD BERNSTEIN

Music by
LEONARD BERNSTEIN

Our Fa - ther, who art in heav - en, Hal-low-èd be Thy name. Thy king - dom come,

Thy will be done, on earth as it is in heav - en. Give us this day our dai - ly bread

And for - give us our tres-pass - es As we for-give those who tres-pass a - gainst us.

And lead us not in-to temp-ta - tion, But de - liv - er us from e - vil. A - men.

When the thun-der rum - bles, Now the Age of

Gold is dead And the dreams we've clung to dy-ing to stay young Have left us parched and

old in - stead, _____ When my cour-age crum - bles, _____ When I feel con-

fused and frail, _____ When my spir - it fal - ters on de-cay-ing al - tars _____ And my il-

Tranquillo
(No breath, if possible)

lu - sions fail, _____ I go on right then, I go on a -

cresc. un poco

gain. I go on to say I will cel - e - brate _____ an-oth - er day... I go

(non arp.)

Mommy, are you here?
(Dede's Aria)
from A QUIET PLACE

By
LEONARD BERNSTEIN
and
STEPHEN WADSWORTH

Hey, I sound like Jun - ior. ____ Why not? Af - ter all... ____ ha.

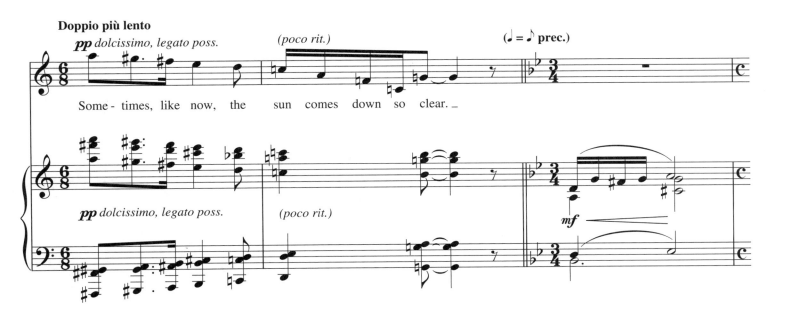

Some - times, like now, the sun comes down so clear. __

I've been afraid
(François' Aria)
from A QUIET PLACE
original key

Music and Lyrics by
LEONARD BERNSTEIN

ma con moto, quasi agitato

I've been a-fraid,　　　and ver-y much,　it's true.　　But

now ___ you are here and I　know _____ I'm not a-fraid. ___　　That ___ I can

need _____ you　and I can have　you too.　　*Et ce dè - sir, _____ ce dè-sir ne me*

(laughs, shrugs)

Con moto (come prima)

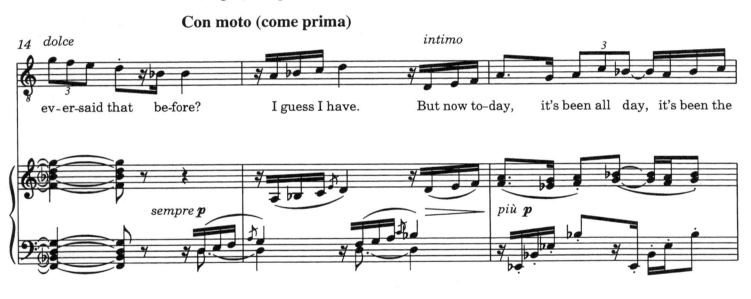

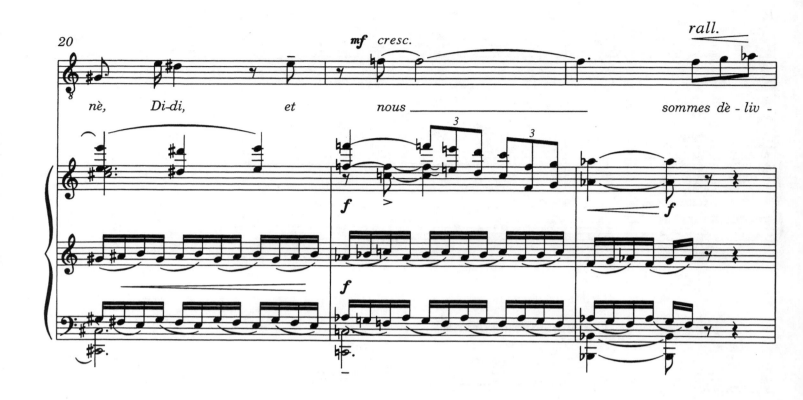

Poco meno (♩=69)

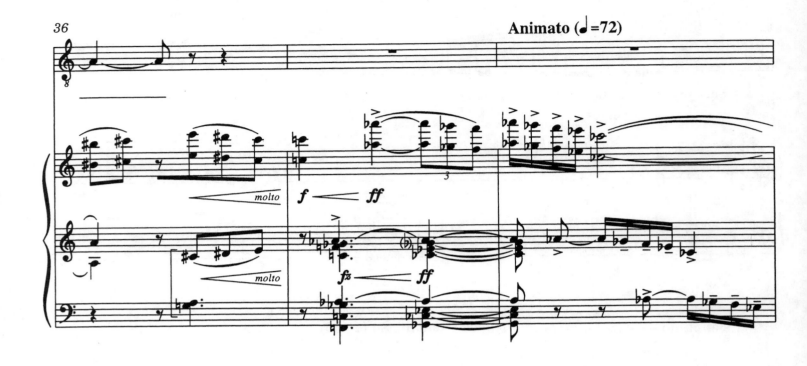